'Ye Cannae Shove Yer Granny Aff A Bus!'

SCOTS GRANDCHILDREN ON THEIR GRANNIES

Allan Morrison

ILLUSTRA

www.vitalspark.co.uk

The Vital Spark is an imprint of
Neil Wilson Publishing
303a The Pentagon Centre
36 Washington Street
GLASGOW
G3 8AZ

Tel: 0141-221-1117
Fax: 0141-221-5363
E-mail: info@nwp.sol.co.uk
http://www.nwp.co.uk/

ISBN 1-897784-81-3
Typeset in Bodoni
Designed by Mark Blackadder
Printed by Cromwell Press

Contents

✳

With thanks to many grannies and the children
of Ravenscraig Primary School, Inverclyde.

Introduction

*

'If it wisnae fur yer granny, where wid ye be?' goes the old song, and how right it is. When I was growing up grannies seemed small, squat individuals, all dressed in black with hemlines an inch from the floor. They sat by the fire, darning socks, knitting woollies and nagging grandpa for smoking his pipe in the house.

Traditional Granny ...

Today's grannies are somewhat different. They are into Highland dancing, aerobics, healthy eating, mini-skirts and SAGA holidays in the sun, and they still keep grandpa right! But they do have something fundamentally in common with the grannies of yesteryear. They ADORE their grandchildren!

Scottish grannies, (or grandmas or nannies or nans, if you prefer), with their strong family ties in Scotland, are quick to relate their grandchild's latest achievement, and the wonderfully funny and witty comments

... now into Aerobics

Iron Age Granny

they can make. In my first book, *Haud Yer Wheesht!*, the wise observations of generations of Scottish grandmothers were recorded and venerated. Now it's the turn of their offspring's offspring who, no doubt, through the vibrant genetic pulses running in their veins, believe that from the age of two until nine, they must give the world, and their granny, their own insights and observations on life.

After all, they are the next generation of poets, writers, entrepreneurs, explorers, inventors and politicians who, by their unique Scottish character, continue to significantly shape the world.

16th Cent Granny

Look out, Scotland, here they come !

Stone Age Granny

Did You Know That Scottish Grandchildren..?

Are the smartest children in the world!

Are the funniest children in the world!

Are little people who tend to see the world in black and white. (Due to the Scottish weather!)

Have no inhibitions, which gives them a head start on the best adult intellectuals in Scotland!

Did You Know
That Scottish Grannies..?

Are filled with wonder that their own children, with
all their faults, could have produced such
remarkable offspring!

Are usually capable of talking the hind
legs off a donkey, but are reduced to baby talk
with the new arrival!

Are experienced journeymen in the art of child
rearing. After all, parents are just apprentices!

Are amazed that they are now old enough to have
grandchildren!

Think that youth is a wonderful time. It's just a
pity it's wasted on children!

Are folk to look up to regardless
of how tall you grow.

Hold their grandchildren's hands
for a little while and their hearts for ever.

Some Famous
Sayings On Children

'Train up a child in the way he should go,
and when he is old he will not depart from it.'
King Solomon

'Grown-ups never understand anything for
themselves, and it is tiresome for children to be
always and forever explaining things to them.'
Antoine De Saint-Exupery

'There are two things a child will share willingly —
communicable diseases and his mother's age.'
Dr Benjamin Spock

'You know that the beginning is the
most important part of any work, especially
in the case of a young and tender thing; for that
is the time at which the character
is being formed.'
Plato

'Never give a child a drum!'
A Scots granny

'Childhood candour…shall I ever find it again?'
Leo Tolstoy

'There is nothing thirstier than a five-year-old
who has just gone to bed.'
A frustrated Scots granny

'One of the luckiest things that can happen
to you in life is to have a happy childhood.'
Agatha Christie

'Anybody can be a parent, but it
takes a special person to be a granny.'
A Proud granny

'If I had known what fun grandchildren are,
I would have had them first!'
A Glasgow granny

'Youth is wholly experimental.'
Robert Louis Stevenson

That Special Relationship

*

A grandchild has something in common with a visitor from another planet or someone from an unfamiliar and exotic country. Seen for the first time, a land like Scotland with its exciting and stimulating opportunities, together with some pretty interesting occupants, demands that observations and questions

THAT SPECIAL RELATIONSHIP

emanate from the young traveller through time. And who better to direct these questions and remarks to, but the person who would do anything in the universe for them. Granny!

Parents should be a child's first guide, but they are busy and harassed people. So God supplied an army of grannies who provide endless patient, sensitive attention to the varying moods of their grandchildren. And grannies are fiercely proud of all their grandchildren's achievements. Remember the tale of the Inverness granny phoning the doctor? 'Doctor, doctor, please come quickly! My grandson, who is top of his class, has cut his knee.'

However, granny may sometimes feel she has a rival.

fiercely proud of all their
grandchildren's achievements...

'*Ye Cannae Shove Yer Granny Aff A Bus!*' is a well-known song in Scotland, but it does raise the question of inter-family relationships. Remember the words?

Ye cannae shove your granny aff a bus,
Oh ye cannae shove your granny aff a bus,
Ye cannae shove your granny, for she's yer
      mammy's mammy,
Ye cannae shove your granny aff a bus.

You can shove your other granny aff a bus,
You can shove your other granny aff a bus.
You can shove your other granny, for she's yer
      daddy's mammy,
You can shove your other granny aff a bus.

The song was probably written by an upset daughter-in-law, or indeed by a granny none too keen on the opposition! Scottish grandchildren are therefore very fortunate. They have hardly arrived on this planet and people are already vying for their affections!

something in common with
a visitor from another planet...

The 12 Key Granny Rules for Grandchildren

1. Always listen to their wee stories.

2. Have enlarged photographs of them on your wall and in your handbag. (OK so buy a bigger handbag !)

3. Read them fantastic stories. Compose some of them yourself. They'll love stories about their parents when they were young.

4. Have a lucky-dip bag available for them when they visit. Fill it with such things as 'freebies' from cereal packets.

5. Make plenty of clootie dumpling.

6. Have some toys and books which stay at your home in readiness for their visits. (*Oor Wullie* and *The Broons* are timeless favourites.)

7. Follow their favourite team.

8. Half live in McDonalds!

9. Give them pocket money every week. But they must come to your house to collect it!

10. Send them postcards every time you are away somewhere for the day.

11. Ensure that they know 'the rules' as to how they should behave. Praise them and reward them for obeying these rules.

12. Tell them you love them every time you see them.

The 12 Key Grandchildren Rules for Grannies

1. Always tell granny everything funny that happens to you. She just loves to tell your wee stories to everybody.

2. Always give granny a big hug when you meet her.

3. Remember to send granny a birthday card with lots of kisses on it. (Grannies are never older than 45!)

4. Do your very best at school. Tell granny everything you do that is clever. They just love to brag to their friends.

5. Stay overnight at granny's and keep her company. Sleep right through the night, and don't have mummy and daddy having to come to collect you at 3.00 o'clock in the morning!

6. Learn granny's favourite song and sing it to her.

7. Draw a wee picture of you and granny
   for her to put up on her wall.

8. Always send granny a postcard
   from your holidays.

9. Learn a poem by Robert Burns and
   recite it to granny.

10. Sing to granny all the songs that you
    are taught by your teacher.

11. Take your wee pals round to see granny.

12. Send granny a special card at Christmas...
    made by yourself.

1

...On Education

Granny trying to get wee Susan,
age five, to improve her counting:
'And what comes after six, dear?'
'The Scottish news, Granny.'

Granny McLaren enquired of her
five-year-old grandson, Duncan, if his
teacher was older than she was?
After much hesitation he said, 'Well Granny,
she disnae have as many cracks
in her face as you do.'

Two wee girls talking in nursery school.
'My mummy won't get me a Teletubby doll
for my birthday. She says they are too dear.'
'Och, just ask your Granny. She'll get you
anything you want!'

'Granny, can you help me with my homework?'
'Sure, darling. What do you want to know?'
'If someone cuts a tomato into four pieces and a
cucumber into ten pieces what do you get?'
'A salad!' says granny with a giggle.

The teacher said to five-year-old Jane,
'So you've got a new baby sister, Jane?'
'Yes, Miss.'
'Do you know Jane, I'd like a baby too,'
confided the teacher.
'Oh, it's easy Miss. All you do is have a bath,
put on a clean nightie and then
send for Granny!'

'If my teacher was like Granny then
she'd be nicer to me.'

Granny asked wee Diana. 'And what's your
favourite day now that you're a big schoolgirl?'
'Saturday, Granny.'

Granny to Robert, age eight.
'What would you like to be when you grow up?'
'I'd like to be a big alsatian!'
'Is that so you could scare everybody?'
'Yes.'
'Even your teacher, Mrs Macdonald?'
'Not her. Nothing would frighten her!'

'Granny. A wee boy in our class has German
measles and he's only been to England.'

'Granny', moaned a tearful Annabel.
'The wee boy at the next desk says my
name's awful funny.'
'Right!' said granny. 'I'll go and see
your teacher and get this sorted out.
What's his name?'
'Mustapha Singh, Granny.'

*

Mark, age eight, was told by his granny that
if a girl teases you at school then she
really loves you.
'Well Granny,' said Mark, 'thousands
of girls must love me!'

Proud granny, who fancies herself as a
bit of a soprano, to grandson Iain.
'You know. I've been singing since
I was nine years old.'
'Is your throat not sore yet, Granny?'

'Granny helped me with my spelling words
homework and I got one wrong. I told Miss Aiken
that Granny had helped me. But she said it was OK
as Granny hadn't been to school for years.'

'Granny, I'm never going to be able
to learn to spell.'
'Oh, why not, George?'
'The teacher keeps changing the
words every day.'

Stephen told his teacher he had never
heard of Robert the Bruce. He explained
that his granny had told him that
'If they've no' bin on the telly,
they're no' famous!'

'Granny. I don't like the school.'
'Why's that dear?'
'Well, Granny. I can't write, but I'm quite
good at talking, and the teacher won't let
me talk and just wants me to write.'

'We got gym at school today, Granny.'
'Oh, can you stand on your head yet, son?'
'No Granny. it's too high up.'

Concerned granny to eleven-year-old Alan.
'Alan. Were the school examination
questions awfa' hard?'
'No Granny, they were OK. But the
answers were really difficult.'

Granny was at the school sports day and was
holding five-year-old Brian's hand as they watched
his elder brother in the egg and spoon race. Then it
was Brian's turn to run in the sack race.
'I'll run, Granny, but I'm no' goin' to
wear wan o' those big goonies!'

2

...On God, Heaven and the Angels

*

Linda was sitting quietly drawing,
and granny enquired as to the subject.
'I'm drawing God, Granny.'
'But listen, Linda. Nobody has ever seen God.'
'Well, they will now!' announced Linda.

*

Sandra, age nine, was being tested by
granny for the forthcoming Sunday School
examination on the ten commandments.
Granny asked. 'What commandment do you think
of when you think about your mum and dad?'
'Honour your mother and father.'
'Good', said granny. 'Now, what commandment
do you think about when you think
of your wee sister?'
'Thou shalt not kill!'

Granddaughter Hazel was seated next
to granny, right at the front of the church.
The minister's sermon was in full flight.
'And what would you say if I were to offer
you anything you wanted in the
whole world?' He boomed.
Hazel said. 'Yes, please.'

'Every year everyone has a birthday
unless they're with Jesus!'

'Granny says we will sing hymns to
Jesus in heaven; but He doesn't
take a collection!'

'Grandpa has gone to heaven to live with the angels, so Granny has gone to the bingo.'

'Granny, where is your Daddy?'
'Oh, he's in heaven, Paul.'
'Do you go and see him?'
'Well, it's a bit far away.'
'How did he get to heaven?'
'God came and collected him.'
'Wow, what kind of motor
does he have?'

Three-year-old Craig was in church, and his granny told him that this was God's house. He looked around and asked, 'Where does he keep his telly, Granny?'

Jack had been in church for
a half an hour or so of the service,
when he tugged at his
granny's sleeve and enquired.
'Can I have an ice cream at
the interval, Granny?'

Exasperated granny to grandson, Gordon.
'Gordon, I believe that you think I was
born at the time of the Ark!'
'Well Granny,' said Gordon. 'You do seem
to know an awful lot of dead people.'

'Granny says that dogs don't go to heaven as
they'd spoil the pavements made of gold.
Should God not give them golden grass?'

'My Granny says that God is always with me.
He doesn't need any sleep.'

Granny was in church with grandson,
John. She showed him the war
memorial plaque on the church wall.
'These are the names of those who died in
the three services,' she explained.
'Oh,' said Ian, 'I thought there was only
one in the morning and one at night.'

'Grannies are old and go to heaven quickly;
so you have got to be nice to them immediately.'

'Grandfathers go to heaven early to buy
mansions for the Grannies.'

'Mummy says that the minister is the only
man who can keep Granny quiet for an hour!'

Granny was telling wee Hugh, age three,
about her pending trip up the west
coast with grandpa.
'We're going to Skye,' she said.
Hugh immediately burst into tears.
'Don't go up to the Skye, Granny.
I don't want you to die.'

*

Stephen was bored in church listening
to the minister's sermon and turned
to his granny and asked.
'Granny, are you sure this is the
only way to get into heaven?'

3

...On Birds and Animals

Young Jack welcomed granny's friend's
big black dog by giving it a big hug.
Then he pulled out his tube of Smarties,
threw them all on the floor and said.
'Right Oscar, take two!'

'My Granny says that her wee Westie,
Penny, has a birthday every year;
but Penny doesn't know this.'

'Your nose is cold, Sandra,' said granny.
'It's a sign of puppy love.'
'We've only got a wee cat, Granny.'

Granny and her five-year-old granddaughter
were looking from the window into the garden.
'Look Hilary,' said granny.
'Isn't that a lovely bird?'
'Yes Granny. It's a robin undressed.'

Granny's wee dog was sick and she
told grandchild, Luke, that they must
take Snowy to the vet. She also explained
that a vet was an animal doctor. Luke
thought for a moment and asked.
'Granny, will the animal doctor
be a dog or a cat?'

Granny and granddaughter, Christine,
were discussing hens, eggs and the
tricky subject of reproduction.
'Granny.' asked Christine. 'Did you lay
Mummy before you laid Uncle John?'

'I gave our dog, Rory, a bath, and Granny
cleaned me up afterwards.'

'Granny. We saw a man on Largs pier
drowning worms on a bit of string.'

'I love my dog and my Granny the
bestest in the whole wide world. But Cindy
smells different from Granny.'

'Granny's wee dog , Bonny, is a great watch-dog.
If Granny hears a noise, she just wakens
Bonny and he barks.'

Granny had wee Adam on her knee and
they were talking about animal noises.
Then granny was inspired.
'What do you think a rhinoceros says, Adam?'
'Peep, peep!' said the confident Adam.
'How's that?' asked granny.
'It's got a horn on its nose, Granny!'

Granny to granddaughter Elizabeth:
'Are you the teacher's pet, Elizabeth?'
'No, Granny, she's got a wee kitten!'

'Granny, my mummy is like a bird.'
''How's that, Ruby?' asks granny.
'She says she's got to watch
Daddy like a hawk!'

4

...On Age

Phillip, sitting on granny's knee asked.
'Granny, what did you look like when
you were new?'

Granny was showing a photograph of
herself as a young girl to granddaughter, Mary.
'When did you turn into another
person, Granny?' she asked.

Granny to five-year-old Susan.
'And what would you like to be?'
Susan answered, 'I'd like to be six,
Granny. I'm fed up being five!'

'I am four but my Granny's age is
too high for her to count.'

'When you are wee you add one on to
each year when it's your birthday. That's
because you can't do the takeaways.'

Granny to young Duncan. 'You know,
I remember the day you were born.'
'Well I don't, Granny. I was too young.'

'When I am thirty, and old like Granny,
I will get a walking stick with a rubber bottom.'

'Daddy says that Granny was born in
'the year of our Lord only know when'!'

'Do you know, Claire,' complained granny.
'I've got to the stage where I keep
talking to myself.'
'Well you should just switch
off your hearing aid, Granny!'

'Just look, Susan,' said granny.
'You're four now and you're taller
than my umbrella.'
'Yes,' said the proud Susan.
'And sure your umbrella's
older than me!'

'Granny says she can remember when she was my
age. She has a very good memory.'

'All the babies born in Scotland
are very young.'

'When you are very old, over twenty two,
you don't get homework.'

'My Granny says that you get weaker
every time you have a birthday. I'm getting
very weak' said six-year-old Jemma.

Granny complained to her granddaughter,
Susan, that she was getting old.
'It's OK, Granny,' said Susan.
'You just need your face ironed a wee bit.'

5

...On Christmas

Three-year-old Diana was helping granny put
ornaments on the Christmas tree.
'Granny', she said. 'Sure Jesus was lucky
to be born on Christmas Day. He would get
birthday presents and the
ones from Santa.'

Motivated by visiting a nativity scene,
young Ronnie was prompted to ask,
'Granny, who was Jesus' Granny?'
'I don't know, darling,' said the
stumped granny. 'Why, didn't you know
her, Granny?' 'No I didn't.'
'Were you just a wee girl then, Granny?'

'Granny, you can do anything
for me, can't you?'
'Of course, Darren, you know
I love you.' 'Could you make it snow,
Granny, as I haven't been able to
go out on the sledge I
got from Santa.'

'Granny, do you think Santa would bring
me a football and an Aberdeen strip?'
asked Daniel. 'Oh, I think that's very likely,
Daniel,' said granny, taking a mental note.
'And do you think he could take away
the piano when he's in?'

Granny was reading the Christmas Story
to Andrew, who was seated on her knee.
She had got to the bit about the Three Wise Men
and the Shepherds visiting Jesus in the stable,
and asked Andrew, 'What do you think Mary
would say to the visitors?'
'This wean cannae get an ounce o' sleep
for the noise you lot are making!'

After granny's two and a half-year-old grandson,
William, had gone to his first Christmas party,
he came tearing into granny's flat to show
her his big red balloon. The next day granny
asked him, 'William, where's your balloon?'
He scowled. 'It's deid!'

'Granny says that Santa will bring me something
nice if I am good. How does he know this?'

Denise brought granny the Christmas
picture she had painted at school. 'That's
a beautiful picture, Denise,' said granny.
'I can see Mary on the donkey. I can see the baby,
Jesus, in her arms. I can see Joseph leading
the donkey. But what's this just behind Mary
on the donkey? It looks like a dot with eight
legs sticking out of it.' 'That's the flea, Granny.'
'What flea?' granny asked.
'Well, Granny,' said Denise.
'In the story, God told Joseph to take
Mary and Jesus and flea into Egypt.'

'My Granny says that Santa will
come down the lum, but I don't
know what a lum is?'

6

...On Food,
Health and
Hygiene

Granny to grandson, Gerry.
'Now Gerry. Soup should be seen and not heard.'
'Don't be silly, Granny. Soup cannae talk!'

※

Tommy, speaking to his hard of
hearing granny at the end of a meal.
'Ice-cream, Granny.'
'Well you shouldn't, Tommy. You'll only
hurt your throat.'

※

'Granny, me no like this ice-cream,'
said two-year-old Doreen.
'Oh, why not darling?'
'It's cold.'

✳

Granny, sucking a chocolate, to
grandson Eric. 'You see, Eric, the problem
is I have a sweet tooth.'
'Which one is it, Granny?'

✳

'Oh, dear. you've lost a tooth, Kenneth.'
'No, Granny. It's OK. I've got it in my pocket.'

✳

'Eat your crusts, Roger.
They're good for your teeth.'
'Did Grandpa not take his
crusts then, Granny?'

Granny was intent on teaching Hugh,
age four, some manners.
'When you yawn, Hugh, please put
your hand in front of your mouth.'
'But Granny, I might get bitten.'

'Granny,' said Nicol. 'Everybody says my
Mum is the best cook in the whole wide world.
Her meals just melt in your mouth.'
The slightly miffed granny countered.
'Aye, well she should defrost them first.'

Granny, educating Rosemary in
the finer things of life.
'Always remember, dear. Stir your
tea with your right hand.'
'But Granny. Ma Daddy uses a spoon.'

'Silly you,' said granny. You've put
your hat on the wrong way round.'
'How do you know which way
we're going, Granny?'

Granny to granddaughter, Hilary
'My ears are burning, Hilary.
Somebody must be talking about me.'
'Well you should put some cream
on them, Granny.'

Granny, to Samuel, age six,
sitting on the dentist's chair.
'Sammy! For heaven's sake say 'ah',
so the nice man can get his finger
out your mouth!'

Granny to four-year-old
Michelle, just before a meal.
'Michelle, would you please sit on my right hand.'
'But, Granny,' protested Michelle. 'How are you
going to hold your knife?'

'Granny, Mummy says that my
wee brother looks like Grandpa.'
'Don't worry dear. As long
as he's healthy.'

Granny to Susan, age four. 'Susan, eat
up your broccoli. It will put colour
in your cheeks.'
'But Granny...I don't want green cheeks.'

Granny to little Rachel, age three.
'Rachel, you shouldn't eat off your knife.'
'But, Granny, ma fork leaks.'

7

...On The Weather

'Shut that front door, Alastair.
It's freezing today,' shouted granny.
'Will it not make it warmer outside, Granny?'

Granny, shouting to three-year-old
Iain who is through in the lounge.
'Iain, look and see if it's raining outside.'
'Granny, I cannae see oot the winda,
but it's dry inside.'

Granny to wee grandson, Fraser, who is lagging
behind her somewhat on the pavement.
'Hurry up, Fraser. It's raining cats and dogs!'
'Granny, I can only see wan wee dug.'

'Granny, have you got lots and lots of money?'
'Well, not really darling. But I'm
saving up for a rainy day.'
'Are you going to buy an umbrella, Granny?'

✳

There was thunder and lightning
over the City of Aberdeen and granny
told wee Lorna there was nothing to
be frightened about.
'It's OK, Granny,' said the calm Lorna.
'Daddy says it's just God clumpin'
aboot takin' photos.'

✳

'My corns always know when it's raining'
announced granny to Lynne.
'How's that, Granny? Do they get all wet?'

'Quick son', said granny, 'it's raining.'
'If we go quicker will it rain less, Granny?'

Granny and grandson, Kevin,
has been out shopping in the rain.
Granny sat down wearily and said:
'My knees seem to be getting awfa
stiff these days.'
'Maybe it's just rust with
all the rain, Granny.'

8

...Answering Granny's Questions

Joyce, a sixty-one-year-old widowed granny,
had just got engaged. Her seven-year-old
grandchild, Nicola, asked her when the
wedding day would be. She smiled coyly
and said, 'Well, we can't afford it just now.
We'll need to save up.'
'It's okay, Granny', said Nicola,
'your Daddy pays for it!'

Granny asked her six-year-old grandson,
Andrew, who was taking Scottish Country
Dance lessons, what his favourite dance was.
'That's easy,' he replied. 'Strip the widow'.

'Guess where I was away to today?'
granny asked granddaughter Lynne.
'My Mummy said you were away
doolally, Granny.'

Granny McCorkindale was visited
by her grandson, William, and his
three-year-old pal, Charles.
'And what's the name of your
parents, Charles?' she enquired.
'Mummy and Daddy.'

Alexander, staying overnight at granny's
house with his brother Christopher,
(a notorious bed-wetter!), was asked
by his granny which end of the double
bed he would like to sleep in.
'The shallow end, Granny' came
the smart reply.

Jill's grandmother was teaching her
manners. 'When we want something we
always say the magic words, please may I have?
Now, what are the magic words, Jill?'
Jill replied, 'I love you Granny,
and abracadabra!'

*

Granny , giving her precious little
granddaughter, Margaret, a cuddle.
'And how do you think I was lucky enough
to get you as my granddaughter?'
'You must have been first in
the queue, Granny!'

*

'When my Granny gets angry and asks
me if I think she came up the Clyde on a bike?
I don't answer, but just give a wee smile.'

9

...Asking Granny Questions

*

Eight-year-old Julie to her granny.
'Granny, when do I get HRT?'

*

'Why do the flowers stay in beds
all the time, Granny?'

*

Nine-year-old Maureen asked her granny,
'Granny what's it like to go out on a date?'
'How should I know,' replied granny.
'Ask your other Granny.
She's the wan wi' the fancy man!'

*

'Granny, where do fire engines
take fires to?'

*

'Granny, do storks really bring the babies?'
'Of course, Pet.' 'Well who brings the
elephants, Granny?'

Granny and Sadie were talking about
what Sadie would do when she grew up
and how much money she would earn. Sadie
suddenly asked, 'How much do you get
paid for being a Granny?'

'Granny, how is it that cows eat green
grass and give us white milk?'

'Do chickens get chickenpox too, Granny?'

10

...On What Granny Says

My Granny says '…chew food forty times
a mouthful. But it makes my face sore.'

My Granny says'…she was out for a wee dauner.
But I don't think she bought one.'

My Granny says '…my mother is priceless.
I think about five pounds.'

My Granny says '…I must have been
born upside down as my nose always runs
and my feet always smell.'

My Granny says '...that I have a big
imagination and a big head. But she kisses
it all the time.'

My Granny says '...you can smile a
thousand smiles every day. But I can only
count up to about sixty.'

My Granny says '...my hair is a mess.
She knows what she is talking about.'

My Granny says '...grandpas snore
like old trains.'

My Granny says '...more with one look,
than Mrs Henderson could say in a week.'

My Granny says '...I'll break my arm patting
myself on the back for being so good.'

My Granny says '...not to tell wee fibs. But
sometimes she does!'

My Granny says '...she doesn't walk a lot
now at her age; but my Mother says that
Granny's mind still wanders.'

My Granny says '...you should always wear
clean underwear in case you're in an accident
and have to go to the hospital.'

My Granny says '...I must have been born
in a tent, when I forget to shut the door.'

*

My Granny says '...she keeps
her age under her hat.'

*

My Granny says '...I'm going to be
a doctor when I grow up, because I
never come when she calls me.'

My Granny says '...if I don't brush my hair
properly I look like an accident waiting to
happen. I don't understand her.'

My Granny says '...Mummy had her babies
young. I've never seen old babies!'

My Granny says '...that children of five
know all the questions, and children of
fifteen all the answers.'

11

...At Granny's House

Granny to grandson, David, age three,
at breakfast. 'And how did you sleep
last night, dear?'
'With my eyes closed, Granny.'

Granny to Louisa, 'Now how many
times have I told you not to be late?'
'I don't know, Granny. We don't get
adding up until next week.'

'Granny peeled onions and I cried.
But I wasn't sad.'

Fraser was ill and staying at granny's house
while his mum was at work. In the afternoon
she asked him how he was feeling.
'Granny, I'm feeling better but my
bottom's still sick!'

Four-year-old James had stayed overnight
at granny's house and after breakfast he was
sitting on granny's knee getting a wee cuddle.
'Sure there's nothing better than your
old Granny, son', said the doting granny.
'Oh yes there is!' 'And what's that?'
'A granny with sweeties!'

Granny had made a special meal for wee
William, but halfway through the
scrumptious food he burst into tears.
'What's the matter, ma' wee pet?' asked granny.
'Granny, I'm fu' but I'm no done!'

Granny to wee David: 'You know David,
you're lucky. Santa doesn't come to
my house.' 'Why not Granny?'
'Well, you see, no boys or girls
stay at my house.' 'OK then Granny,
I'll give you ma' wee sister.'

Four-year-old Joyce, was having tea
with Granny when she noticed an old soup ladle
hanging on the wall. 'What's that for, Granny?'
'Oh, your Grandpa used to use it for soup.'
'He must have had an awful
big mouth Granny!'

A Wee Mixture

*

Granny was teaching four-year-old,
Elizabeth, to count. 'What's two and two?'
'Four, Granny.' 'What's two and three?'
'Five, Granny.' Granny gave her a hug
and said, 'You are wonderful.'
'No, I'm not,' said Elizabeth.
'I'm fantastic!'

*

Granny said to young Tom.
'Give your Granny a big kiss.'
'Granny', said Tom, 'I've given you fourteen
already and they are all done.
Try again tomorrow!'

*

'When my knee was sore my Granny kissed it
better. Then she gave me money.'

'When I grow up I'm going to be like
Granny and live in a conservatory
with a lounger.'

'My Granny gets up three times during the
night to make tea for her and Grandpa.
I told Granny they should drink the tea
before they go to bed and they could
just sleep all night.'

'Granny's friend says that you can
tell when children are growing up, when
they stop asking where they came from and
start refusing to tell you where
they are going.'

'I love Granny. She and I like cuddling teddy.'

'My Granny always smiles. Except in the morning
when she doesn't have her teeth in.'

'Grannies should get prizes for being nice.'

'My wee brother's nappies would put you off chips!'

'I got lost in Tesco's and couldn't find my Mum. I
was a wee bit frightened. I would never have got
lost if I had been out with Granny.'

'Granny, my wee brother wet the bed.
I've never wet the bed. Well, once.'

'My mummy says that Granny has eyes in
the back of her head. I've never seen them.
They must be under her hair.'

'I like to whisper in Granny's ear. I've got to
speak into the right one as the other one has
broken down.'

'My Granny makes a lovely hot tin of soup.'

'My Mummy says I don't need
make-up at my age. But Granny lets
me use her lipstick.'

'My Mummy always says that she won't
give me pudding until I've eaten everything
on my plate. But Granny just gives me
the pudding anyway.'

'Granny it's no' fair. I cannae tell any wee
white lies when I'm looking at you!'

'When I grow up I'm going to have a nice
Grandpa, like Granny has.'

'Mummy says I've always got to love
you and be nice to you, Granny.'
'That's really sweet, darling.'
'Yes, she says babysitters are too expensive!'

Granny and granddaughter, Pauline, were
in the toy department of a store in Edinburgh.
'Granny,' said Pauline. 'Can you buy me
this dolly here. It walks and talks and when
you put it in its cot it shuts its eyes and
goes to sleep, just like a real baby.'
'Oh, aye,' said granny. 'I can see you don't
know anything about real babies.'

'My Granny is fat because she has
had more birthday cakes than me.'

'I made Granny laugh when we watched
'Blind Date', and I said, I don't fancy going
away with him for a week!'

'Granny's wrinkles go away when
she's not laughing.'

*

'Daddy says that Granny is an auld antique.
But antiques are worth a lot.'

*

Granny to grandson, Ian, age seven.
'And what are your mum and dad getting
up to this weather?'
'I don't know, Granny. They keep
spelling a lot of words.'

Granny arrived unexpectedly at her daughter's house and immediately apologised for coming empty handed. 'It's OK, Granny' said wee Sarah, 'you've got your gloves on.'

'Granny says that Grandpa has only got a wee bit of hair so he doesn't need to wash it much.'

'My Granny is not as old as she looks.'

*

'My Granny was born in Clydebank, and the next day the Germans tried to drop bombs on her, but they missed!'

'Although my Granny takes out her teeth
every night she doesn't get any money for
them in the morning.'

'My sister and I went with Granny to see the Queen
in Edinburgh, but she wasn't in. My Granny says
she must have been out for her messages.'

Granny to Amanda. 'Now Amanda! Your
Mummy never told lies when she was a wee girl.'
'So, when did she start, Granny?'

'Granny has a sore back and Grandpa told her it
must be with carrying stories. He is a silly
man at times.'

'My Granny tells me all the bad things that Daddy
used to do when he was a boy. He was a very bad
wee boy, but Granny loved him.'

Proud granny was pushing her new twin
grandchildren through Bon Accord Shopping
Centre in Aberdeen when she was approached by a
little girl who looked in the pram and enquired.
'Where are they joined, Missus?'

'How about you and me singing a
wee song together,' asked granny.
'OK, Granny...let's duet.' (Well that's
the way granny reported it!)

Granny, to her visiting
granddaughter's friend, Freda.
'And can you play the piano too, Freda?'
'I don't know, Mrs MacDonald,
I've never tried.'

Granny was proudly playing her
new keyboard to grandson, Simon.
'Of course, Simon, I can only play by ear.'
'But you're using your hands, Granny.'

So What Is A Scottish Granny?

'Grannies are people who protect
children from their mother and father.'
Rose, aged 10

'A granny is a person who lets
you stay up late and eat her wee cakes.'
Kim, aged 8

Grannies are folk who give your
knee a kiss when you fall.'
Bert, aged 6

'Grannies are people who give
your teddy a cuddle.'
Rosemary, aged 6

'Grannies are people who let you
slip into bed with them when
you are cold and scared.'
Mary, aged 6

'Grannies sing in the kitchen!'
Simon, aged 8

'Grannies are always twenty-one even
if your mummy is thirty-two.'
Stephen, aged 11

'Grannies are kind of soft to sit on.'
Sally, aged 5

'A granny always knows when you've
been bad even when you don't tell them.'
Lorna, aged 8

'Grannies know all the answers,
except how old they are!'
Stephen, aged 11